Pim and the Mat

By Sally Cowan

Sim and Pim sat.

Sim is at the tap.

Pim is at the mat.

Pim! Pim!

The mat!

Sim sits.

Pim pats.

Pat, pat, pat.

CHECKING FOR MEANING

1. Who sat with Pim? *(Literal)*

2. Where was Sim? *(Literal)*

3. Why do you think Pim pats down the threads in the nest? *(Inferential)*

EXTENDING VOCABULARY

sat	Look at the word *sat*. Find two other words in the book that rhyme with *sat*. Can you think of any other words that end in –*at*?
mat	Look at the word *mat*. What do you do with a mat? What else can you sit on?
sits	Look at the word *sits*. What is the base of this word? What has been added to the base?

MOVING BEYOND THE TEXT

1. Do you think the threads from the mat would make a good nest? Why or why not?

2. What else can nests be made from?

3. Why might Pim be building a nest?

4. Birds live in nests. What other types of homes do animals live in?

SPEED SOUNDS

| Mm | Ss | Aa | Pp | Ii | Tt |

PRACTICE WORDS

Pim

Sim

sat

tap

at

sits

mat

pats

Pat

pat